PROFESSOR HARRIMAN'S STEAM AIR-SHIP

PROFESSOR HARRIMAN'S STEAM AIR-SHIP

Terese Svoboda

EYEWEAR PUBLISHING

First published in 2016
by Eyewear Publishing Ltd
Suite 333, 19-21 Crawford Street
Marylebone, London W1H 1PJ
United Kingdom

Cover design and typeset by Edwin Smet
Author photograph by Joyce George
Printed in England by TJ International Ltd, Padstow, Cornwall

ISBN 978-1-911335-18-4

*Eyewear wishes to thank Jonathan Wonham for his
generous patronage of our press.*

*The editor has generally followed American spelling and punctuation
at the author's request.*

WWW.EYEWEARPUBLISHING.COM

A recent Guggenheim fellow, Terese Svoboda is the author of six previous collections of poetry, an opera, a biography, six novels, a memoir, and a book of translations from Nuer. Currently teaching at Stony Brook/ Southampton, Svoboda has twice been Distinguished Visiting Professor at the University of Hawaii and has held the McGee Professorship at Davidson. She has also taught at Williams, Sarah Lawrence, Columbia School of the Arts, College of William and Mary, Bennington and many other institutions.

TABLE OF CONTENTS

We play until Death calls us in.

– Kurt Schwitters

I

WHOSE LITTLE AIRPLANE ARE YOU?

Clouds not dragon but plane
                                       explain why apricots make
disappointing peaches, I think. I had not counted on
                           so little apprehended, looking out
                                    the window that stands
so much for self I shut it when another opens.

                   All I claim are fingerprints,
         whorls peculiarly the sum of no experience
but that jerky moment
                   when the egg gets it.

             While we were living on Ludlow,
I say, that was the time of those clouds and your bottom
         with hair on it so apricot
             it should have been bitten. The clouds were not ripe and the
planes –

             Let me look out the window.

THE TALKING TEA-KETTLE

It's a tea kettle, not teapot, the vessel
        you boil water in, not the steeper. This one whistles

when it's ready,
           it commands your presence,
               mocking your impatience with its steam.

        To hear voices makes you schizo.
To hear the dead makes you socially unacceptable.
           To hear the dead speak from a spout barely hot
is interesting.

      Mom – are you listening?

            The magician David P. Abbott,
          whether he invented the trick himself
or not,

        filled the kettle with plain so plain Nebraskan water
        and the subject stuck the spout in her ear as if
she hoped for a steam cure.
               Telephones
were not widespread then, that any object
        should emit messages had the currency of new tech
           those in the know approved,

                  people with enough money to conjure
their mother's final final words, even otherwise wise men, even
      millionaires
pursued this magic,
            the anti-death gesture, the adventure between
        something
and nothing.

We are the teapot, steeping, wondering what to ask:

Where did you put the million dollars?
Do you forgive me?
What about Al-Qaeda?

It's been a hundred years since magicians
                                        routed mediums
like bad angels from the kingdom of heaven,
from the kingdom of magic.
                        Mom?

A magician decapitates me
            on a sidewalk in Nairobi. A scarf around my head, a tug.

Of course I see nothing. Everyone screams.

                        Mom! I want to speak to Mom.
                        I'm over here, Mom, dead too.

        Then I'm not.

Houdini outed David P. Abbott's tea kettle trick
then Abbott joined Houdini's quest
                        to root out the spirits, those returned via
a medium, by definition
                        in between.

Take the trance state. Take suggestion.
Take knocking on wood
and children hidden
under the medium's skirt,
take a third leg beneath
            the table,

                                   slates flipped overhead,
notes passed —

Ah, notes. That they might fall from the beyond
                            with just the right message:
        You must marry
        Miss Bang
                      writes the dead infant,
        Miss Bang being the medium conducting the séance
and the groom,
a soon-to-be millionaire widower.

                            Do the dead change their minds
                            and tell all, or just report — *I'm so happy.*
                            Do the dead care?

                                    Mom?

'I have always felt that if the spirits of the departed could return to
us mortals, they would not require a tin horn to talk through, and
the entire absence of light-waves in the room.'

                                                David P. Abbott

He solved every riddle the mediums posed
                            but after he died
                            his manuscript with all the solutions

was left in a pile of trash
made by the new owners
of his
    Omaha House of Mystery.

Burnt,

it would be smoke.

Who saved his book,
who commanded it to be pulled from the fire?

I never could talk to Mom.

Why we don't believe in mediums now
has less to do with debunkers
than
with our disbelief in the afterlife.

Magicians we still believe in, our material world
full of here   not here,
tech whirs on it
zero/one, the computer mantra recited
until we're entranced.

Here is the woman's head.
Here it is gone.

THE INJURED FUTURE

The shooting in San Bernardino, Calif. was the 355th mass shooting so far this year.
— NPR, Dec. 14, 2015

The Renaissance fly over the horse's tail hovers, despite the breeze.
The sun's radiance – long dashes – telegraph sunrise or set
the way the center squad, their riders

leaning forward in the epitome of speed, mean
either progress or retreat. The bell ringer on tiptoe
silences the woman-with-open-mouth. She knows.

A last bird's frozen over her, to dive or announce fish, fusion, or fertility.
The forced landscape behind it insists, with palm and cypress,
limes and firs and olives, that ocean will attack where sky

and its dashes go thin. In the farthest corner a single figure,
as lone as his parapet suspended in the perspective,
fixes his grimace, narrowing his eyes to aim.

This is a Christian scene beside the sea of *what next*,
so deathless that white flags flap along the border out of unison,
the visuals of violence, the pull of the frame.

ORLANDO IS US

It's like this: gun gun gun
you're dancing in the back no
front no on the table no
in the Gents sounds like a pop
track sounds like backfire
firing then he laughs shoots at

no one *the crowd* into it
please please not you crawl
skitter skitter off your heels
floor slick already hit
you closet yourself
mop-first two other guys

mop wounds it's dark sirens
call out shout back you sink
to your knees almost a dance
one guy breathes loud one guy
pees fear crouches outside gun-

ready what if they hit dark in
that closet you can only outside
touch bullhorns music plays
on music enters time
enters you tick tick you're
losing it tick to the floor tick

a bomb blast lights the tick
a vehicle groans sheetrock smoke
a single no shots loud a man
at the closet a fireman
hatchet help you cry
you fall into his arms

GRIM SLEEPER

– The LA Times' name for the serial killer who took a twenty-year break.

O what is that sound – a shot in the night?
Down in South LA, a shot, then a round?
Only the cops, practicing for a fight,
The cops, clowning around.

O what is that shadow I see – just the toes –
next to the dumpster, that look so cold?
Only the trash, my dear, an old pair of hose,
twisted, dirty, covered with mold.

O why are these women being murdered again?
Why are these women now dead in a ditch?
All those years, my dear, then a change in the brain,
some kind of irresistible itch.

Why haven't they arrested the neighbor?
Why haven't they sent out an alert?
Why don't they pull out a lie detector?
Why are none of them experts?

O is it the white dude they want,
is it the white dude? Is it?
No, the white dude's run off to Vermont
so the judge can't issue his warrant.

O it must be the coked-up cop caught with a prostitute –
though he died before the new murders began –
that will be a bit hard to prosecute.
Now they think it's a married man.

O what are they doing with our son's DNA,
what are they doing with their chemistry?
Only the usual, dear, for the catch-of-the-day,
or perhaps they're hoping for efficiency.

O where are you going now? Stay with me here.
Were the vows you made out of nothing?
It seems I'm not such a good liar, dear,
I must be leaving.

O our locks are broken, the door is smashed,
O the intercom's screeching, screeching.
They're throwing our grandkid's toys in the trash,
and their eyes are burning.

NEIGHBORHOOD WATCH

A weather of sweaters mostly moth-woven,
tea made from tires you find as rags on the road,
toast you'd rub on your skin and draw blood.

What's outside the front door could be your first boy.
Just a bird, so rain-heavy it's dropped past the roof.
The half-parked car won't open for you

until you scratch a word into its window-grit:
Want, of course, a planet telescopically
positioned on *On*. You hobble off,

your cheek withering for kisses. Take the iPad
with its easy interface. Our face, you say,
staring at its black. Boot it up.

WAZIRISTAN

'We're not darkening the skies yet', says Richard Christiansen,
the NASA subcontractor, 'but we are poised.'

Doodlebugs over St. Paul's – whine, then smash,
the V 10 quick to drop death
so impersonally.

Why start with the English?
Matthew Arnold, the droning clash
at the cliffs
infrared across the darkling plain,
God at the controls from an off-site screen.

Enhanced i
is not Please.
The Pakistani in the photo bears
what's left, silver shards.
He disappears (we disappear him).
Ditto his wife. And the photo –

Cornfields buzz with toy Predators
that slice
the sky over our waving grain
for weed,
or for immigrants. FDR: *We are descended from*
immigrants and revolutionists –
remember, remember always.

Birdwatching – except it bags you.
Soon they fly en masse,
flocks smarter and bigger
than ever.

There's a cave ahead.
Think Morlocks.

                      All day, four of them weighting the sky,
the brain.

                With seraphim flinging fire,
       who needs air?

No wonder bombs
               try
       Times Square.

BAGHDAD CALLS

At the market where
Is that a melon? is
discerning, with bloody

not-melon still
spurting
in that silence,

even the big birds,
market-bound,
do not dive.

After the living begin
wailing, collecting
in the shade, before Help

has strapped on what
wings it has, the ringing
begins, every cellphone

flung from pockets
without torsos, from
fingers without purses,

their *Are you safe?*
stilled by someone
parsing the parts.

HOPE WANTED ALIVE

A blood-faced lion raises its maw.
I could be in the supermarket, Saran Wrap thrown back on chicken,

instead there's *Hope Wanted Alive* scrawled along
the mud-slick side streets

where kids roll bottle tops, kids hawk one seed of what?
In Nairobi the slum starts where I stop, gallery-bound.

Forty children in clean costumes of show-off
purport to live in the two rooms abutting the paintings.

You could drink the sugar cane at the end of the street
or you could set fire to it.

I did see truck tires without trucks.
I did see ice cream nobody would lick

and slits up the side of a dress,
and always huge knives that cut,

in my case, canvas. A big painting
not in celebration of our president

but the blood-faced lion, looking
for the supermarket, kids in claws,

bottle tops for eyes, nobody costumed
who isn't running, politicians

with outstretched arms equaling
– or trying to – hope. I buy it.

ORPHEUS

...the trees moved close to shade him, becoming creaturely...
Michael Schmidt, *The First Poets*

In case anyone is wondering, the river road is closed.
In case anyone is wandering, a geranium's lost blossoms cross the asphalt.

No, that's drops of blood against the black. The river will rise to sluice it,
and since someone's assigned fish and birds thinking souls,

it's easy to explain the waves' origin: plate movement, china plates,
think Japan, an anime of someone just tsunami-ed.

We'll just wait, we'll just stop all the tooth-brushing and money-gathering
and folderol and sit here to wait-and-see, you-and-I, you being

really too squeamish to stop and myself stopping naturally,
poetically, in a skid at the site all gouty.

If you run off, you won't see the waves wash over it, there won't be
a single grimace left by the time the siren-makers swing in,
there will be only the trees, nodding.

But I'll say it if you won't:
the sound it makes is singing.

SETSUDEN

means saving electricity:
turning down the thermostat, no sleep mode
on the TV, clean and defrost the fridge
we accept less power, it means no

Hiroshima   Nagasaki.

Post 3/11 *setsuden* means
walk down the escalator, drink tea
not quite hot, wear sweaters winter
sweat in summer.

Warm Coke labeled *setsudencha*
to honor and respect the greater losses:
those homeless still in Tohoku.

In November 2015 they turn one on again.

Having beheaded the peasant,
the samurai
takes the child onto his horse.

SECOND THANKSGIVING

Endurance, yes. And those high-crowned hats.
But the guest list stays short. Your turn

and turkey, their turn and no corn.
Kids for sure by then, or dead. Always

party with the harvest. But poison in the stew,
on the roast, the squash? Maybe you think

Share. Maybe they think *God's gift,
thanks be to God*. The graves white,

the cornstalks stripped by wind,
the shrieks of those shoe-buckle savages —

Listen: *What spoons to use? Whose daughter?*
Your patience foretold, forsworn, forgotten.

WASHINGTON: D FOR DREAM, C FOR CRUEL

The capitol's spire, that poke-in-the-face,
wards off about as much anti-
as an auntie – know the one? –
always telling jokes about race
that tear straight along the fuse,
a zipping sound, with a cartoon Ha!
that questions "we" until Poof!
no "us" in it either, The End.

This white/black world we're bred to, shoots.
Our finger blown "free"
by someone else on the trigger,
a cat-smile dum-dum,
dud, doofy "free" that means you
don't have to wash it anymore,
a phantom any-color finger,
saluting the one-for-all obscene.

Start over, Red Rover. Don't send
that next body-to-be-counted into our arms.
We're letting race go, the penny says so,
it's God we trust, say it six times: *God reach us,*
Michelangelo's *Yes* instead of *Ha*
and its brothers *Ha Ha*. Hear that thunder?
That's Freedom, cast by 12 slaves and stuck
to the dome – being blown.

RED SUMMER 1919

Josephine Baker, age eleven: Is that a storm coming?
Mother: It's the whites.

After they drag her off the streetcar, black women – many,
on a rampage – hatpin
                              the white girl's blue eyes,
jerk the baby out of her arms,
throw it into the river,
                              then beat the girl to death with their shoe heels.

Whites swim that river as hard as they can, past the corpses,
                              gulping trash water,
              while blacks shoot them like carp.
Some make it across –
                              to black kids who stone them.

Whites, wounded, try the door, any door. Inside, blacks
clear the table to pray.
                                        Outside, a wild mob shouts:
Out or we'll set you afire.
They turn them out.

The ambulance drivers leave the wounded white man
to be thrown into his own burning house.
                                        Except black is white.

1917. Ida B. Wells' report stayed sealed until 1986.

East St. Louis.
You ever hear of East St. Louis?
Not St. Louis.

A place grown too fast filled with Southerners
fought over then left to the boll weevil.

                                   Boll weevil stew.

There's trains that stop in St. Louis, there's work
                          since the pacifist President talked up war,

there's unions trying to exclude the blacks.

                                   Whites
cut the fire hoses, shooting blacks who fled the flames.

                          I don't care who started it.

10,000 marched in NYC, the men in black,
the women in white – all races – in memoriam.

So?

        64 lynchings the next year.
                          Then Red Summer.
We have Commies to blame for that, agitators
                (who needed agitators?)
in new blue cotton workpants to hide behind,
not men disguised

        in white peaked sheets, and
let's not forget (we have not forgotten)
                 the women who washed the sheets.

An American way of life, a good wage.
(The Robber Barons? Their untaxed undead
        corporate contemporaries?)

> ...black people seeking an industrial chance
> in a country that they have labored for three
> hundred years to make great...
>   – Marcus Garvey

During Red Summer 34 cities burned.

I was naïve, I said our melting pots works,
what's with the Iraqis, the Burmese, the Sri Lankans,
                               all those Africans?

Nobody sent out press releases
on the extermination of Tulsa's Black Wall Street.
                               1921. Oil-rich.
         Bombed from the air with dynamite and nitro,
                  10,000 homeless.

              I've already forgotten the Google
that drew me in:
Negro boy stoned
              for drifting into whites-only water.

Chicago, 1919. The quiet Midwest,
a week of killing.

Did the St. Louis women
pin their hats back on?

II

NOBLE SAVAGE

In 1766, Jeanne Baret became the first woman to circumnavigate the world –
but as a man.

No one remembers her.

Her captain, Bougainville, became the first Frenchman to sail around the world.
He is remembered
by the bush named after him.

The difference between humans and monkeys:
monkeys don't reproduce when there's no food.

Over an island in the Pacific, someone is pushed from a plane.
A woman, just as easily as a man.

A woman falls, was the first to fall.

The plane over water: a dark cross.

After two weeks of sailing Tahiti, Bougainville wrote:
Their only god is the god of love.

What do monkeys dream?
Food, so they can have sex.

Woman on a pedestal, the indigenous as Greek gods –

Bougainville's journal inspired
Jean-Jacques Rousseau's concept:
the Noble Savage.

Bougainville is searching for sandalwood,
that century's equivalent to oil.

As the botanist's assistant,
                    Baret digs specimens,
        hauls big collection boxes on her back.

Women are closer to nature and therefore closer to God, wrote Rousseau.

Only the Polynesians can tell the difference.
                    They sniff Baret when her hands are full.
                            Or are those kisses?

Beware of god reads the sign but there's always barking.

                                        The monkeys bark.

        The plane whines,
                the French journalist plummets,
                        does not miss the island.

Bougainville wrote: *Women pretend not to want what they desire most.*
                    But Baret does not pretend –
she is a man.

What should we do with Baret now? the sailors cry.
Women on board are bad luck.

In dreams you catch yourself, you wake up.

Baret can't watch –
                the Polynesians eat
the mirrors
        Bougainville gave them.
                            How noble.

If we dream, are we guilty?

Or is that a god's work?

A Vietnamese general, interested in oil, pushes her out of the plane.
It is a woman, a woman's body.

She is not remembered.

A fall is always political, a body stands in the way.

We stand on that island, covering ourselves.

This is not paradise, say the monkeys,
say the French, exploding perfect atolls.

What? What? We can't hear them.

They put her off.

Swim, Baret, there's your island.

She reaches Marseilles.

The monkeys eat while someone falls.

GOOD VIBRATIONS

A Theremin is so ugly,
table and post, the performer poking
the air.

But the Beach Boys
make its excitation lap the car

   in rubbery vibrato, rod and cam,
 the beat so, like, everywhere.

Theremin vanished,
– all right, there were KGB –

           but
Stalin executing
   Theremin's cousins still does not wholly
             explain
abandoning his lover,
American fame, and fifties' cash. Patriotic duty?

I am played too,
     in a striped bikini,
the ocean's breath against
the taut string.

Taking the heat, that's something I say
in my bikini,
   the sand burning my belly,
the cops sniffing the air.

       There, at the limits
of mind, of beach, where the sand is so fine –

I hear it —
                    horror movie music.

I think: Brownian motion:
if the particle is very small,
          the hits it takes from the heat
of another
                    causes it to jump

Wrong. I turn on my towel,
                    idle and mortal and clueless,
the song fading,
the waves pawing the sunset,
          sound equaling light at some speed

until there is the intimation of something,
          or better, an irritation —

the first rain that stings.

GREEN GIRLS

Wriggling on the bottles:
Drink us, drink us,
green girls

tell you water
is the long hair that you
swallow.

Whistle all you want,
a girl who swims this water
will make you swallow in the dark.

But if you tell her no,
(Not no, not no,)
then water's all you've got.

Lonely on a rock
the green girls do their writhe,
Drink me, drink me –

it's dark inside,
inside the inside,
deep inside the green girls.

There's a thirst inside
the green girls
you can't wait to find, no,

running down your windshield
coming from behind.
They're nymphs

you'd like to drink,
Drink us, drink us.
Oh the green girls want to die.

Down the drain, down –
help us, help us down the drain.
No one knows what's inside.

It's dark inside,
inside the inside,
deep inside the green girls,

there's a thirst inside
the green girls you really
want to ride.

EZ PASSITIS

All six lanes of love, driving, driven off,
all sex lanes. But I thought

I made that turn. The sign said:
Like as not. Like a snot. Love's

tender buttons' picked, aureole-
plucked on a media tacky with smut,

with a two-highway hum. Ahem.
Signs give at a given speed. What gears

there are get put through the ears,
snowy with left petals petioles

petit mort of some smegma
magma of the act, median to

where every carload rubbernecks,
crawls the whole length of.

He or she or not loves you.
Get off, have the body checked

& checked. A mirror finish.
Love as not. Not as love.

AIRPORT NEWS

                                  Crating Virgil,
medicated solemn and soon whisked
        into darkness,
                you relinquish shoes, identity, water.

Dante-esque instead of picturesque –
        the murmur of TV, the unboxed grease filming
        the chairs,
                nerves playing nerves,

the murmur of women about insecurity,
        dusk repeating dawn
on wings frozen in the mid-flap
of promise,
                roar efflux from the porcine jumbo
don't look now   belly white
        inflated
                with seats –
you are swallowed.

The cell rings. Beatrice. Looking forward.

You watch
        birds float in the exhaust,
                        birds
winged with wing-nuts,
                        sheet metal noisy,
whose suns swarm from them in dazzle,
cold suns
                Virgil would shake his shaggy coat
in soft mouth retrieval for,

tarmac be damned.

Waiting, ascend a circle.
                    The controllers,
really only one exhausted courier
who is messaged
                    with what we can only
infer,
                    his ziggurats riven with lightning, computers
too bright then black, an *Oh!* of light after,
                              a rain of zeroes, death worked
to a shine. Why not

put this circle on hold,
put it in your breast pocket where waves
                    of electricity
                              will converge on your heart?

There's lift anyway, and the usual efforts unfold;
the landing gear as the withdrawing
                    privates, pale men cornering boys
in window seats,
                    the mile-high club
                    annoying the movie-drawn coke-swilling lines
of aisle-standers,
                              surely a circle unto themselves.

Gluttony is next, the second bag of nuts,
                    more drink, a cooking show that displays
even the skim saved from the fat,
                              the pork
of nothing to do but eat.

                    Politicized,

you see cabin-ward, through the eye-slit

                           of the first mate

       the ice
of rough cloud.

              With a cargo of slaves
working the turbines, and albatross

stabbed to the plane's nose, you sense loss.

                 But you don't beat on the windows,
turn off the cooking shows,

                 or step out and stretch.

Wait, wasn't that the tower? someone cries
               while contrail writes
      its peanuts of ellipsis,
the plane dusting itself in seeming advertisement.

       The lights redden, the pilots yawn,
                 smoke after sex –

you presume, their door being inviolate,
      their circle untried, their authority a god's,
             the perfect stewardess primping
       a la Beatrice in the galley.

                 Then terror, that fallen angel,
lights, as if another service. Two rows up
       the grumpy hero wraps his hand in towels,
the body's stowed in the bathroom,
             grave inconvenience. Better this

than tossed in a vat of blood and fire,
          fiery flakes raining from the sky of
Play. You curtain the window, hit it.

A demon with red wings
appears onscreen, Game 1.
Keep to the right,
sings the adolescent next to you.

                        This level's got circles
and seething shit,
            creatures headfirst in holes in rocks,
sorcerers with their necks on backwards,
                        boiling pitch –
you're losing points –
            and a guy named Evil Claws.

You load up with leaded cloaks (for X-rays),
snakes and lizards, a Trojan horse, and sail off
to hack the Sowers of Discord.

Satan, all three faces of the races,
laughs.
            Surely he hovers
                        outside the porthole. *Save.*

You feel a sudden deceleration, a plunge, the *Wait!*
that gravity insists. Upright your seats, please,
            it's showtime. You prepare to land,
                        nuts in palm,
arm
            on the single armrest
            of intimacy, all profiles
                        facing forward
where, in horror-movie
            or Lolita-bound tension,
the cabin-mongers
            Cross check!
                the reliquary moment.

You do descend Satan's furry back,
ascend and descend.

To park
at the wrong gate where weary souls
trip over rubber guides? Not yet. *I'm sorry*
the stewardess says

into the cirrus of jet exhaust
defining the moonscape of every airport,

nests of screens everywhere
communicating the con of flight:

We'll be another ten minutes or *It's just a small part*.

Virgil! Virgil!

He answers with a whine from the hold.

Here, that's
what they're selling, *There*,

distance so close
the breast tips drag –
how long can the stewardess keep her neck
arched like that?

The clouds themselves circle, and fast.

They could be sharks
with wings, the view darkens so.

Skimming

the omnivorous boil,
gods, more than one,
stir the mess
until Beatrice is borne aloft,
gate-free.

She waves and putti clap.
     Smart-assed
thinly clad lads, they do not remain seated,
                                        they gyre
          up one stair flight at a time.

The bouquet she's holding – the bride's – gets sucked
                              into the updraft
roses,
          orchids,
                         lilies
coming apart
                              as unimpenetrable
                              as an entire flock –
                                        the plane stalls.

          Next comes paradise.

ODYSSEUS'S MOTHER-IN-LAW

Oakum seals the gaps as if a boat would talk,

                                people go down

to the very close walls of it and sniff

and row the seams with more oakum and the ocean

dares not make a sermon of it,

though the boards be not as tight as an old woman,

                          the old woman complains

up and down the deck, and further, that microwaves will wave

right through it, saying the hellish part –

not the *Thanks for the tip* part –

comes later, after the rainclouds and the crossed

        swords, after the embassy

darkens its doors

and the corsage hits the ground –

all that

she personally knows about,

being old.

        Seek and ye shall destroy, he says.

She says *the afternoon at least is young.*

Why Penelope waits and weaves

                   instead of scouring the known world –

        It's not like

you've covered your tracks.

Oakum, he persists.

The hullish part.

A small green item rolls out of her,
could have rolled out. Mortal.

Hold my sea-bit hand.
If party
                isn't what we set out to do
then you should go home, she says.

She makes a tap, tap, tap, tap
on the aluminum hull that should bob
the breakers oakum-less, that should not mind any,
indeed, should vanquish, all waves.

It's not like we're going anywhere.
Sweetheart, she says

proving her own heart still beats,
and the waves.

On her pins now, she says he will catch
        some secret-bearing animal,
one sealed and wrought,
and then what?

I won't, he says, and pushes off.

                Watch for leaks,
she says, the tide knitting and un-knitting
its jetsam, almost tea leaves in a tea cup against the seashore,
        the wind like a coming-apart companionway.

He turns his head into it.

Tangled in line, a corsage drifts by,
all rubbery blooms,
   with the smell of diesel,
 red green red.

GLASS OF WATER ENCOUNTER

She dances only in her necklace,
scotch-lit surely. He touches his glasses.

Nightie-less, dugs whipping, hair sprung,
some music inside, out, wet tongue

tip at her lip, no mere palsied shuffle,
both boney feet lifted, elbows awful.

Shakespeare's banshee of wailing parts,
a woman with hair, a woman with warts.

He's fixed to the floor. Dear Abby:
do other presumed-sane mothers get ghastly,

wait in the dark after the ball
to strip for their sons at the end of the hall?

A dream, insists his sister
but his first wife knows better.

MOTHER DOESN'T BITE

I bite instead and she needs salt,
a little more time on the grill.
Young men are coming,
they'll want her.

Her head is an oyster
turned out of a shell.
She needs her rocks,
and wave after wave.

Dumbstruck, I crest
but her claws position me,
ready for the knife. But who
holds the light?

The young men laugh.
It's a game, it's fun, it's everyday.
I run across the beach,
a toll at last tolling.

Gulls rise with her eyes,
They shriek, night
iced under their wings,
its salt falling.

THANATOS MACHINE

You don't need a machine to do that.
A plastic bag will do. But he built it,
his tools cast about in the unit
while he got up his nerve to use it.

Nothing more was stored there.
A poured cement floor, a triple-locked door
after door after door down a corridor
reeking with the odor of everything over.

In heretofore phrases, he left a note
outlining his *Help!* in argot
so wrought it was hopeless to ferret out
his intent, meant or not.

A ball-peen hammer was all she had.
The shards cut her. What else had he hid?
At least, she cried, he'd thought ahead,
and drove halfway home instead.

WHY WANE, WHY NOT WAX?

A line on my computer screen
equals an EKG of a bus bounce –
okay, I dropped it – signals

that its seeing will falter, its bits
break on a faux horizon
of oughts and ones slamming

into whatever sand silicon
comes to, dead. Express it
better as an exchange,

as a continuum, that train of *ums*
with engines on both ends.
The computer upends

and its gold gets chucked out
in China and re-circulated,
despite deadly fumes. Such a vision

strives to see Linda's cancer
as a new way. Call it
Gethsemane, Golgotha,

all the glottal hesitation at
the abyss – but A is what we start over with.
Like how the Beatles

funded the first CAT scan –
an engineer invented it
on their royalties after

EMI made it big. Keep it
all return and rhythm,
a groove that plays to the center.

DEATH MARCH

Carry her the way it has to hurt:
arms outstretched, tears caught.

Shrimp-curled, she weighs a shell's worth.
Worse, no nurse lurks.

The flag's furled in every way –
she whispers *Go Away*.

Reality singes.
A Cortez

she made you, no piker –
at every conquest, anger

you needed to guy
yourself to her bedside.

Muscles, pectoral or invented, signal
terror – you can't put her down. Moral

imperative, that of social stigma
probably Darwinian, militia-

ready, beats its chest. The gods are plural
and cruel. You won't weep at her funeral.

You wait, the dark doesn't, it presses down.
You can't possibly walk. Then it's dawn.

CANED

A stick, pared clean – no, a silver topped
bamboo-with-dagger, class doubling as club,
the advantage of gravity lifted high
overcoming the disadvantage of poking ahead.

He demurs. Weakness either way.
A man should crush opponents with a word.
Naive, I muse, at your age. A cane
replaces the sole's sensors, bolsters them.

Balance is a matter for the unbalanced,
he says, all nuance, accusing me, Lear-lover,
of too much. The earth is now close, I tell him.
A sharp look. I'll walk, he says, without.

BOY ON CRUTCHES

Every third car in the lot shines silver-with-roof-rack.
You press your goose-caller but nothing honks back.

It could be broken or the car could be on 6. Wait here,
you tell him, his tick-thud echoing after

your every wrong turn. You ran two stops
to make his appointment, then you abandoned ship

willy-nilly, the waves licking, the waves
of concrete rising as the elevator misbehaved.

Every pew is filled on 6, all is silence.
No attendant, with god-like countenance,

just a family plodding with such purpose toward you,
asmirk at your obvious idiocy. You

go back for the boy but it's the wrong bank.
Did he wander out or go game-deaf? Thank

god, on 9 the key fits, 9 is the 6, comics face down
in the back seat. You cruise 3 for him, done

with panic, your head thrust so far out of the car you almost hit
a post. Instead, you graze advertising and sit

in *Park*, you pen the stall number on your palm, you call and call:
only columns answer. He's at the exit. By that time you're al-

most crying, most un-dad-like, slipping, with blinks,
the ticket into the quick mouth for its automatic thanks.

DARK DADDY

The dark daddy went about the hushed place in a turncoat. *You can suspender him,* said the allegator, the one alleging that such a dad wasn't Good-For-The-Planet, that such a dad had better watch his feet in said place. The place pivoted and the dark daddy went down. *Are there flames? Is there fissure?* cried — instead of said — the allegator. For that, a chorus strode in, in interjection. *Halleluia,* they chorused, hoarse the way the word makes you, and loud. Nobody heard what the dark daddy said as he bent even lower to do what? *Bent? You bet he's bent,* said the allegator. The hushiness of the place shrugged off their silence — the chorus, the allegator, the dark daddy doing what? spotlighted in clamor. The rasp of metal, the screech of chalk, the of of of. The place pivoted again, nobody could hold it, the allegator and the chorus keeping their footing by shrieking, a technique all instinct. The dark daddy never got himself closed over, he just went darker, bent over. *Where are the chains we ordered?* the chorus raved in ascending arpeggios. The allegator announced too loud: *He left his coat.* Together they rent it into twos and threes until all that was left was the hush.

COUNTESS LETHARGY

The countess eats sunlight for breakfast.
Dogs slink around her bed in hunger.
Lest you make sacred her image
on a brick, in your drive, or thumb,
she needs to be turned twice a day,
plantlike in her déshabillé.

Lethargy has its roots in lethal.
This is the sadness
you must share or die,
the waves over your head,
the waving you're not doing.
Pride vacuums away the scraps

yet nobody empties the bag.
Maybe she hurts. Maybe.
The dogs devour her at dusk.
You have it in a book, read once,
now on the computer shelf.

Clever is what those dogs become,
touring monsters punished
by huge crowds anxious to see
the countess' soul fly – bird! – from their mouths.
She wears gold and shines: sunlight.
You are one of those dogs.

III

Professor Harriman's
Steam Air-Ship

A time will come when our descendants will be amazed
that we did not know things that are so plain to them.
— Seneca, Book 7, 1 CE

PROFESSOR HARRIMAN'S STEAM AIR-SHIP

I.
The Coming Mode of Travel from New United Monster
Railroad Shows Circa

Invent the air first, then trees, then wood,
then the fire inside the ship, steam wavy,

the canvas-covered wings
Verne-ing the fantasy forward,

> a headless goose mid-flap,
> a douche of smoke to suggest progress,

> > man aft, standing at the levers,
> > his eyes fast on the woman

> > astride the command post in boots,
> > skirt hiked to her haunch,

> > > steam building. She's all about
> > > ringing a bell hung from

> > > the neck of the bird-horse
> > > she straddles. *Professor!*

We're so modern
our mag-levs fly our guideways,
magnets
creating both lift and thrust

only a few inches over
leveled air.

Yet our tech still plays their tech:

                              Sugar Easy X-ray.

Transportation as transport:
               Court-ship.

II.
[Invention of] Conception

A calliope sounds.
O shipped air, roars the show.

Theatrical *in extremis,*
she scarves herself so the eye's

drawn beyond the premise of
all that air holding him to her.

He wedges a stovepipe hat to his ears,
heating the space between crown

and head. Shuhplattling
the night before, he slapped shoe to hand.

                        She flew first,
       both feet in the air.

61

Above
the lonely crowds: we we we we we

To fall and see oneself falling.

Audubon's twisted-neck birds,
their wings pinned so life-like, flying,

unflocked,

the dead black eyes
viewing gravity.

Gravid already, that we.

III.
The Tender

The Professor wipes his glasses
on his pants. He's bare-chested,
chopping wood. Hairy-man.

All men. The rope for mooring
tangled from stretching it
from end to end of the machine and her walking,
such a princess,
across it.

She spits, she spurns.
Desire buttons its Off,
no naughty in this aeronautics.

Then the air goes ashy: motes.
It hits them —
that's why she cries and he has red eyes.

Argument makes them married, there's lead
in the hem of her hiked skirt.

The Jetsons
       sideways-coast toward us. Idea
is all we need, the present streaming the future.

Medtronic manufactures
a genome that attracts
DNA to bone,
the Gee Whiz of reproduction,
its right-to-life
writ on computer code put somewhere safe —
the air —
       some call it cloud.

       We breathe it.

IV.
Gee Whiz Code

Inventors pile their rucksacks
at the door where they deem the steam
air-ship useless. Experts in atmosphere
decry the presence of humans in clouds
and the making of clouds,

other experts mustache themselves
with condemnation read as envy
by the rest. No one will try it
rhymes with *buy it*. The ship dodges
chimneys. Does she kick at the brick?

Some inside come outside
with their theories, wings and sun and wax.
Disarming their invention-weapons,
Harriman's beauty unpacks the *why* in them:
Commerce is betrothed.

The Future is robed, we're all too fat
                                    for Spock's synth shirt.
                    Wherever we aim our lasers, there's crystal,
                                    the endless answer to structure.
                    But shoot
                              and there's the Buddhist reverberation
                                    of a bell gone off, mirroring
                                              the tintinnabulation in our heads,
                    of all that invented elsewhere
                              we yearn to be part of.

V.
Blueprint for Tree, as in Family

You haven't seen a tree
until you've seen
its shadow from the sky.

— Amelia Earhart

Blue and red glued to the wall,
    wind-ripped

                scribbled-on broadside:
    they float off.

Our robes,
in disrobing,
    will make all the noise
in the probable cold of the Future
        except for
    the O we make with our lips,
the Dear *after.*

VI.
So Many Miss The Spectacle

                                    the sky was cloudy
                                    or they were beating flax
                                    for a shirt, or they were cold
                and just didn't see,

                                    lying on their backs
                                                    after berry-picking,
                    or asleep beside the hedge,
                                    their children tugging.

                    25 cents to contribute kindling.
                    25 cents for souvenir silk.

            Frightened people pay to watch
                    what frightens them.

The future isn't about the grief of the present.
Holy Moly — it's the saints
turned to stone, each generation marooned
                            in the smoke of Babel,
                                    the Wright idea gone wrong.
                            Yet to have flown!

VII.
Clowns

So long do they dangle over the rooftops,
TV antennas, dishes, cellphone towers appear,

their bup-bup-bup rethinking
the rhythm they're dancing, the method by which
babies
        occur too much too often too late, whole towns exploding.

They are too deaf to hear the failing chug,

            the ship
gasping, the tent tops frozen below
                        (haven't they gone anywhere?).

    They roll together

while the clowns
lean back, pointing up,
            their big feet weaving under their taut circle,
first near the gate, then in the street.

Death watches,
the passenger they took on
to empty the ashtrays.

Does she disembark on the 23rd floor of the new skyscraper,
        skirting the bare plates
of township and farmland and cloverleaf?
                    Does he argue *body weight*?

If one of them
steps off first, the ship will land more lightly.

For the innocent children who whispered so excitedly
Outside the locked door where they knew the presents to be
Grew up when it opened.

                                    Auden

VIII.
Carrying Capacity

A single story is like history-in-the-making,
no note from another floor explains
the one you're on – once through the door,
in and out of rooms, terraces, courtyards:
the 19th century so bright with mechanics,
the 20th electric with crackle,
the 21st locofoco with sun –
where Yours turns into Ours.

Rusty boiler.
Torn canvas.

All the trees cut.

We are not yet birds.

IV

IT NIGHT WAS

Will night never come? — Samuel Beckett, *Waiting for Godot*

No one imagines
night at noon. Especially

night as a bus
without words, stripes,

or symbols, carrying us
into more dark noon. Grey first

the white noise of day,
a winnowing of

particle bad/wave good,
a cross-country, yawn-stiff

rice-mush day that designs
out self. Stay wicked,

with a wick. The bus presses
the everyday full sun

into the half-moon orange,
presses the air around it,

presses it flat. We don't
look, our look is strictly

See? I never
thought I would.

CIRCUS FOR A SMALL BOY

The window was high, its ledge low.

I did not arrive in time,
                              inside time,
safe
          inside it.

Instead,
a skidding ambulance –
                    that circus,
its scream-awful ahhh –

(Time folded, a napkin around a fly.)

First, the stairs, so many stairs
                              coiled,
so many of them in the way
circling down,
down
          – draining water –

to be run down.

          Did my hand brush his on the ledge?

                    Like a bag of laundry to the
woman
whose car deflects
                    his feet
so his head hit –

BODY MOSTLY FLOWN

A De Chirico head aslant on a coverlet,
body mostly flown, the dazed prayers dumb.

The ritual cigarette, the ritual drink:
incense, holy water. No ambivalence,

the insides fled, the whispers
of tenderness – mine – he's deaf to.

He's in that corridor, tunnel, the light is left on –
shut it off. But the nurse has to see the thermometer.

No ambivalence. No valence either, no speech.
My heart stops, skids. No lingering regret or all,

sealed with stubbornness, forgiveness
for a life less fairytale,

the hard breathing still, still.
A wing flaps and fear scurries out,

a mouse with a crumb it meant to eat earlier.
De Chirico empties the portico.

THE DAY MOTHER CRIED

Word bubble suspended, an Xmas ornament,
everyone in bits in reflection, maybe
even thought, a confluence of broken glass
and not enough light. Baby *Os*

almost a pucker, could it be a kiss?
Faux night/day/night in answer. No elves.
The "justs" arrive. Repeat is one thing,
another is Dad behind the paper,

or Man. The dog chews off the front page.
Qualms in the kitchen, the dishtowels balled,
the ham incense, prayer someone drops
into the forkfuls, the air cubed hard.

FREUD'S CONTAINER

I'm always boarding –
that is to say –
I'm ticketed and
there's a line and
maybe you go first,

someone small with
the scent of damp skin,
soft hands, limbs
thin. Always
we're happy

but anxious,
the line isn't
moving, the ticket
isn't right, the gate's
detumescing.

The plane flaps
its wings and loss
arrives, an egg
we step around,
boarding

but there are no
seats. We forgot
the seats! I have to
fix all that went before:
ticket, line, egg

but it's too late:
someone small to whom
I've said *I'll be right back*
is left inside
and flies.

ON THE ANNIVERSARY

Drips off icicles
           reshape the sand
      where the driveway's bare —

           the movie coughs,
the one where he's so young.

There's a pullback, the drive
                runs into a spring-high river,
      the sand is a dune of salt,

many dunes.

     Ring-ring!

            Over and over:
the same call, the ice, the drip.

The light never
fades like that again, the car
motor stops in such silence.

      But there, outside the frame,
is where he did die
not yet five,
falling all three floors,

         nothing movie about it.

      Touch that triangle *Play*.
Touch it.
Touch it.

HEADSTONE

The gingkoes mate over the sidewalk
where his name lies scrawled – or did.

Rounding the block, I find
jackhammers at the rundown rectangle

scored with his childish print.
Stop, I plead *Stop*.

But two chunks with severe edges
already jut up, conglomerates of chipped stone,

and other kids hesitate at the truck
sluicing the new cement

in forms like Legos, their names
already grit on their fingers.

PIETÀ

Okay, she's sad but too young, his lover, or maybe a sister,
and she can't get a grip on him – he's sliding off –
and she hasn't bound his wounds. Not even a rag.

If he's really dead, all the bleeding should be over. If he's not,
she ought to do something. No. She's sad. Her stone eyes suck
at her dread, cold and hard. Your son dies

and you want to rip out your hair, you attack the guards,
you scream no matter how often He told you
it would come to this. You don't sit and stare

like a lover or sister, biology pending –
His blood dripping out is yours. If you'd only said *No*
to the angels of orgasm, if only you'd died sooner

you wouldn't have this weight on your lap
carved from the same piece of marble, its dust already dark
where He's slipped, yourself too old to bear more.

NOTES

The image of Professor Harriman's Steam Air-Ship came from a poster made by S.H. Barret for New United Monster Railroad Shows printed at the end of the 19th century and reprinted on the cover of *Heritage* magazine in the 60s.

See *The House of Mystery: the Magic Science of David P. Abbott* by Teller for additional information on 'The Talking Tea Kettle'.

'Grim Sleeper' is a tribute to Auden's ballad 'O What is That Sound'.

The last two lines of 'Washington: D for Dream, C for Cruel' refer to the many slaves who built the White House, in particular, the figure on the dome of the Capitol cast in 1863 by Phillip Reid, a slave at the Bladensburg Foundry in Maryland. It took a month of work by Reid and other slaves to install it. Reid was freed shortly thereafter.

'Green Girls' is from the libretto for *Wet* that was performed at the LA RedCat Theater in Disney Hall in 2005.

ACKNOWLEDGEMENTS

My heartfelt Big Thanks to Stephanie Strickland,
Eleanor Wilner, Mary Sherman Willis, Steve Bull,
Linda Hartinian, Neil Shepard, Mark Selden,
Neil de la Flor, China Miéville, Beau Beausoleil,
Maureen Seaton, and Timothy Schaffert for their
inspiration, guidance and patience.

The author wishes to acknowledge the publications in which
some of these poems first appeared:

'Waziristan' in *Wolf*
'Grim Sleeper' in *Baffler*
'Orpheus' in *The Yale Review*
'Pietà' in *The Harvard Review*
'Green Girls,' 'Headstone' and 'The Injured Future' in *Plume*.
'The Talking Tea-Kettle as Decapitated,' 'Odysseus's Mother-
in-Law,' and 'Why Wane, Why Not Wax' in *Narrative Magazine*
'Neighborhood Watch' in *The New Yorker*
'Whose Little Airplane Are You?' in *The Literary Review*
'Hope Wanted Alive,' 'Body Mostly Flown,' and 'Countess
Lethargy' in *Poetry.org*
'Airport News' in *Agriculture Reader*
'Noble Savage' in *DIAGRAM*
'Freud's Container' in *Gulf Coast Review*
'Caned,' 'Glass of Water Encounter,' and 'Thanatos Machine'
in *Poetry*
'On The Anniversary' (as 'The View Finder') in *The Awl*
'Mother Doesn't Bite' and 'Death March' in *Plume*
'Good Vibrations' in *Open City*
'The Day Mother Cried' in *Qualm*

'It Night Was' in *La Fovea*
'Washington D for Dream, C for Cruel' in *American Poets*
'Professor Harriman's Steam Air-Ship' in *Fulcrum*
'EZ Passitis' in *The Kenyon Review*
'Dark Daddy' in *Denver Quarterly*
'Red Summer 1919' and '*Setsuden*' in *Salvage*
'Boy on Crutches' in *Slate*
'Baghdad Calls' in *Al-Muttanabbi Street Starts Here* (ed.
Beau Beausoleil and Deema Shehabi, PM Press).

 **EYEWEAR** PUBLISHING